Salt Lake City

Rocky Mountain Wildflowers

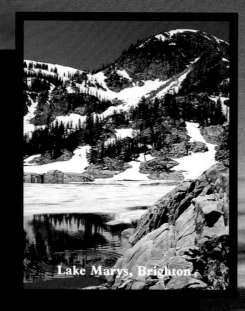

Lake Marys, Brighton

Sunset on the Great Salt Lake

Seagull — State Bird

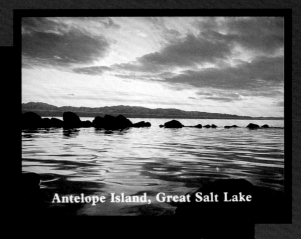

Antelope Island, Great Salt Lake

Sego Lily: State flower

Wasatch Mountains

The Wasatch Mountains contain some of Utah's highest, most picturesque and rugged peaks. They also furnish much of the life-giving water for most of Utah's people, and their canyons provide recreation for more people than any other region of the state.

The Wasatch proper extend about 150 miles from near the Idaho border to Mt. Nebo in central Utah. The two highest peaks are Mt. Timpanogos near Provo (11,750 feet) and Mt. Nebo (11,877 feet); however, a number of other peaks near Salt Lake City also exceed 11,000 feet.

Top:
Big Cottonwood Canyon in the Wasatch National Forest. The scenery in this canyon is striking in its similarity to the Swiss Alps. At the top of the 15-mile-long canyon is Brighton ski and summer resort.
Bottom:
Wasatch Mountain Canyon above Olympus Cove in Salt Lake City.

This is my yard.

Bottom:
"The Greatest Snow on Earth" — 40 feet of it each season — is available Thanksgiving to May at seven resorts just 45 minutes from Salt Lake City. The powder snow of these Wasatch range resorts is the deepest — and most famous — in the world.

Alpine Loop. The Alpine Loop is undoubtedly Utah's most popular scenic drive. Closed during the winter months, the drive is at its best from early summer through mid autumn. *Left: Bridal Vell Falls.* The awe-inspiring double cataract can be viewed from the Provo Canyon floor or by taking a 1,700 foot aerial tramway. *Top: Mt. Timpanogos.* Mt. Timpanogos rises 11,957 feet above sea level and more than 7,000 feet above Pleasant Grove at its foot. The most popular trail to its summit leads from Aspen Grove and takes you 5 miles past a series of beautiful waterfalls, lakes, and the mile-long Timpanogos glacier. *Bottom: Timpanogos Cave National Monument.* Timpanogos Cave is actually three separate caves connected by man-made tunnels. Inside the cave, 1,200 feet above the canyon floor, you'll find hundreds of formations of delicately shaped and colored limestone. The deposits are geologically very young, having begun to form when the cave was at the valley floor several hundreds of thousands of years ago. The cave is open from June through October.

THE GREAT HEART OF TIMPANOGOS

Timpanogos Cave National Monument

Salt Lake City was first incorporated on June 19, 1851, just 4 years after a small body of Mormon Settlers, under the leadership of Brigham Young entered the Valley in July, 1847. It was re-incorporated on June 20, 1860. The City has since grown to a metropolitan area with a population of more than 500,000 people. The City and its suburbs stretch from the Great Salt Lake and Oquirrh Mountains on the west to the snow-capped Wasatch Mountains on the east. Salt Lake City is the Capital of Utah and the State Capitol Building is situated directly up State Street. *Top:* State Capitol. Built of Utah granite on a bench of the Wasatch Mountains, this beautiful Capitol building overlooks the City. Its 40-acre grounds are planted with trees, lawns and great beds of colorful flowers. *Bottom Left:* The nationally acclaimed, Mormon Tabernacle Choir is home in Salt Lake City. Its weekly broadcast from the Tabernacle on Temple Square is the oldest coast-to-coast program on the radio. The 350-member choir, formed 125 years ago, regularly tours the country. Public organ recitals are conducted on the great organ in the Tabernacle. The choir sings each Sunday morning in a performance that lasts 30 minutes beginning at 9.30. The public is also invited to the Choir rehearsals Thursday evenings. *Bottom Right:* This famous monument on Temple Square commemorates the rescue by seagulls of crops which were being devoured by hordes of crickets in 1848, the second year of the settlement. *Facing page:* The world famous "Mormon" Temple and Tabernacle of the Church of Jesus Christ of Latter-day Saints in Salt Lake City. This monumental six-spired edifice took the early Mormon Pioneers forty years to build and was completed on April 6, 1893. Huge hand-hewn granite blocks were hauled by ox team to the Temple site from a quarry twenty miles away. The solid granite walls range from 6 to 9 feet thick and spires rise from 204 to 210 feet high. The east center tower is capped by the golden, trumpet-bearing statue of the Angel Moroni. The Temple is utilized for major religious ceremonies.

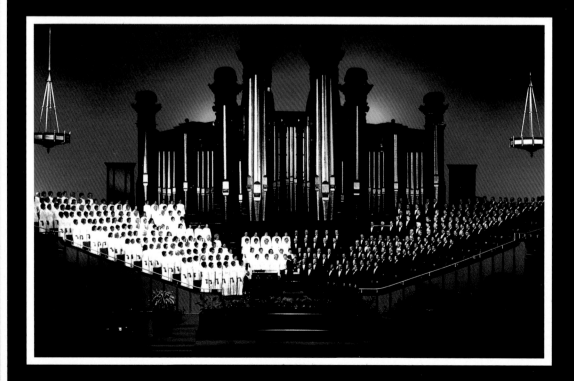

Two mountain ranges form natural borders for the Salt Lake Valley. On the East are the Wasatch Mountains *(top)*. They are rich in minerals and are also used extensively for sporting activities. They are best known for their ski resorts which boast of the "greatest snow on earth".

Right:
The Oquirrh Mountains, which form the western boundary of the Salt Lake Valley, are dotted with ghost towns left desolate after the silver boom petered out late in the 19th century. The Oquirrhs also hold a major treasure of Utah, copper ore from the Bingham Copper Mine. It's the largest excavation in the northern hemisphere, so deep two Empire State Buildings stacked on each other wouldn't reach the rim. The sides of the pit are cut into great steps or benches ranging in widths to sixty five feet and from fifty to seventy feet in height.

The Great Salt Lake, Utah's unique inland sea is located just 20 miles west of Salt Lake City. It is the saltiest body of water in the world (next to the Dead Sea). It is also the largest lake in the United States west of the Mississippi River. Great Salt Lake State Park is located on Antelope Island within the lake. The area west of the lake is known as the Bonneville Salt Flats, the site of the world's fastest speedway.

Bottom:
Bonneville Salt Flats world's fastest speedway. To the northeast of Wendover, Utah, the salt lies flat and hard and dry — the best surface for automobile racing ever discovered. The crystalline salt body that makes the famous Bonneville Salt Flat Race Track covers an area of 200 square miles.
Salt for commercial purposes is harvested annually.

Bear Lake

Pineview Reservoir

Wellsville Mountains

Golden Spike National Historic Site at Promontory, Utah, May 10, 1869.

Autumn Splendor

Devils Slide, Weber Canyon

Logan Canyon

13

The mountains and valleys of Utah offer a never ending paradise for campers, fishermen, hunters, hikers, and nature lovers. Rugged peaks, lush alpine meadows, peaceful surroundings, and clear mountain streams characterize the vast and relatively untouched wilderness of Utah. A few of the many moods of Utah's mountainlands are captured here.

Top left:
Summer Sunset

Bottom left:
Horses in an Alpine Meadow

Top right:
High mountain peaks

Bottom right:
Autumn Storm

High Uinta-Primitive Area has lush virgin forests, clear streams, and towering 13,000-foot mountains (the highest in Utah is Kings Peak at 13,528 feet). The Uinta Mountains, the only major mountain range in North America which runs east to west, are enjoyed by campers, hikers and fishermen who take advantage of the hundreds of snow-fed lakes and mountain serenity. The primitive area is untouched by roads or development. *Bottom:* Mirror Lake is surrounded by 12,000 foot snow capped peaks and pine forests.

Top: The Uinta Mountains are valuable for their water and timber resources, and for recreational uses. *Bottom:* Utah's rugged Uinta Mountains and serene valleys are in beautiful but striking contrast to each other in this North-eastern Utah scene.

Flaming Gorge National Recreational Area
Ashley National Forest

Flaming Gorge Dam, built and operated by the Bureau of Reclamation, is located in the Uinta Mountains of North-eastern Utah. The visitor center on the dam contains displays describing the construction and operation of the dam.

The Dam is a 502 foot high thin arch of concrete blocking the Green River. It is 1180 feet long and backs water 91 miles. Almost 4 million acre-feet of water can be stored behind the dam.

Flaming Gorge

Cart Creek Bridge

Red Canyon Overlook

Sheep Creek Bay

Dinosaur National Monument

Dinosaur National Monument

Only 20 miles east of Vernal, Utah, the entrance to Dinosaur National Monument is surrounded by beautiful scenic sights, such as Split Mountain, and the Green River.

Lower left:
Quarry Visitor Center. Twelve kinds of dinosaurs have been found here in the Morrison Formation since 1909. Today the fossils are not removed but are left in place as a permanent in-place exhibit.

Lower right:
A quarry technician exposes the shoulder bone of a common herbivorous dinosaur, Camarasaurus.

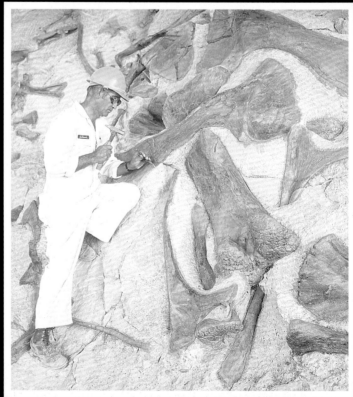

Dinosaur Gardens and Natural History Museum, Vernal Utah.

The Gardens exhibit 14 life-size reptiles, simulating a pre-historic environment.

Top left:
Tyrannosaurus Rex was the largest and among the highly evolved of all the carnivorous dinosaurs. It stood 18-20 feet tall, reached a length of 50 feet and weighed between 8 and 15 tons.

Top right:
Ornithomimus. The hollow-boned ornithomimus is often referred to as the "ostrich dinosaur" due to its resemblance to this contemporary bird. The creature was about 14 ft. long and 6 to 8 ft. tall. With a flat mouth and hard beak ideal for its diet of reptiles, insects, vegetation and eggs.

Bottom:
Brontosaurus. The name Brontosaurus means "thunder lizard" for its earthshaking weight of 30 tons. It is approximately 70 feet long and is one of the largest plant-eating dinosaurs.

Top left:
This scene is in Central-Eastern Utah along the railroad tracks near Castle Gate.

Top right:
The Price River flows through Central and Eastern Utah. Along sections of the river, many varied and beautiful changes in landscape can be seen.

Bottom left:
1-70 in Central Utah is an interesting ride. Many large and impressive rock formations can be seen from the road.

Bottom right:
These petroglyphs were left behind by the Fremont Indian Culture. Nine Mile Canyon is well known for the hundreds of prime examples of Indian Rock Art found there.

Following pages:
24-25 Mount Timpanogos and brilliant yellow quaking aspens.
26 & 31 The Great White Throne in Zion National Park in Southern Utah.
27-30 The Silent City from Inspiration Point. Bryce Canyon National Park.

Glen Canyon National Rec

Rainbow Bridge National Monument

Aerial view

Lake Powell reflections

ake Powell

Glen Canyon National Recreation Area/Lake Powell
Some of the world's most incredible scenic wonders make Utah's Colorado River a definite must. Lake Powell is 186 miles long and boasts an unusual redrock setting. Fishing, camping, boating, "away from it all".

Hovenweep National Monument

Newspaper Rock

The Mexican Hat Rock

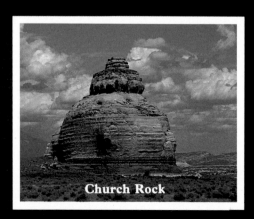

Church Rock

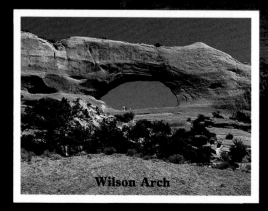

Wilson Arch

**Colorado River,
LaSal Mountains,
Near Moab, Utah**
The mighty Colorado winds past
the LaSal Mountains. In the center
area of the picture you can see the
FISHER TOWERS.

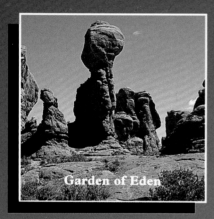

Garden of Eden

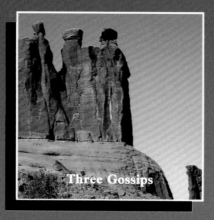

Three Gossips

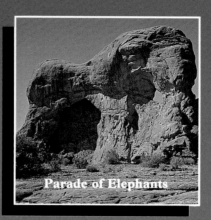

Parade of Elephants

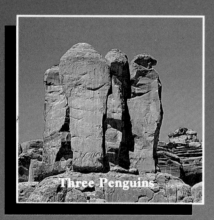

Three Penguins

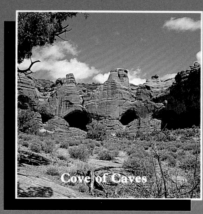

Cove of Caves

Park Avenue Arches

Arches National Park is located north of Moab off highway 191-163. It is the largest assemblage of natural stone arches in the world. The park is a hikers, campers and a photographers paradise.

SHEEP ROCK
One of the many spectacular towers is Sheep Rock, found in the Courthouse Towers section of the Park.

Top:
Double Arch
Arches National Park
The unusual double arch consists of two arches stemming from a common base. The larger arch extends 165 feet from reef to base and towers 156 feet above the debris below. It can be seen from the road in the Windows Section of the park; however, a short walk from the Windows Section parking area allows you to see this beautiful arch more closely.

Bottom:
The Windows Section
Enormous openings cut by the forces of erosion in huge upthrusts of red sandstone, the windows in Arches National Park frame a weirdly beautiful panorama of nature's architectural fantasies. Located in the Windows section, Turrett Arch, on the right, is one of the 89 arches that have been found in the park. The LaSal Mountains in the background are south and east of the park.

Top:
The Spectacles
Composed of the South Window (125 feet by 65 feet) and the North Window (98 feet by 60 feet), this unusual view rewards the visitor who hikes to the far side of the windows.

Bottom:
Delicate Arch
Probably the best known of the arches in this area, Delicate Arch, is considered by many to be the symbol of Arches National Park. The arch is reached by a 1.5 mile hike and is especially beautiful at sunset.

Canyonlands
National Park

Canyonlands National Park received its national park status in 1964. This wild and forbidding expanse of southeast Utah is dominated by the Green, San Juan, and Colorado rivers. Its freakish "slickrock" terrain has often been called a vast wasteland that is impossible for man or beast. *Left:* Angel arch is so named because the figure to the right of the arch has the appearance of a winged, robed Angel. The Arch opening is 190 feet high and 163 feet wide. The Arch standing on a rock wall hundreds of feet above the canyon floor is one of the the world's most beautiful arches. *Top:* Monument Valley is an entire valley created by erosion and filled with many spectacular rock "monuments". *Bottom:* Dramatic rock formations left behind as thousands of years of erosion removed the weaker rock and sandstone are seen everywhere in Canyonlands National Park.

Left:
Paul Bunyan's Potty
A huge ''Pothole'' arch, a few miles up Horse Canyon and the Salt Creek in the Needles District, Canyonlands National Park.

Bottom:
Upheaval Dome
One of the real geologic curiosities of the Canyonlands National Park. Caused by a great plug of salt beneath the surface, the eroded crater in the center is one mile wide, 1500 feet deep. The entire salt dome, the most prominent in the world, measures three miles in diameter.

Top:

**Colorado River from Dead
Horse Point
West of Moab, Utah.**

One-half mile below the vantage
point from which this picture
was taken the River makes a
horseshoe turn. From this point
it is many miles to the nearest
water. Legend has it that wild
horses, crazed from thirst, used
to kill themselves trying to des-
cend the sheer walls to get a
drink of water.

Right:

**Dead Horse Point State Park
near Moab, Utah**

The Canyonlands country as
viewed from Dead Horse Point
offers a special treat with the
dark red sandstone in constrast
with the winter's snow and
clouds.

Natural Bridges National Monument

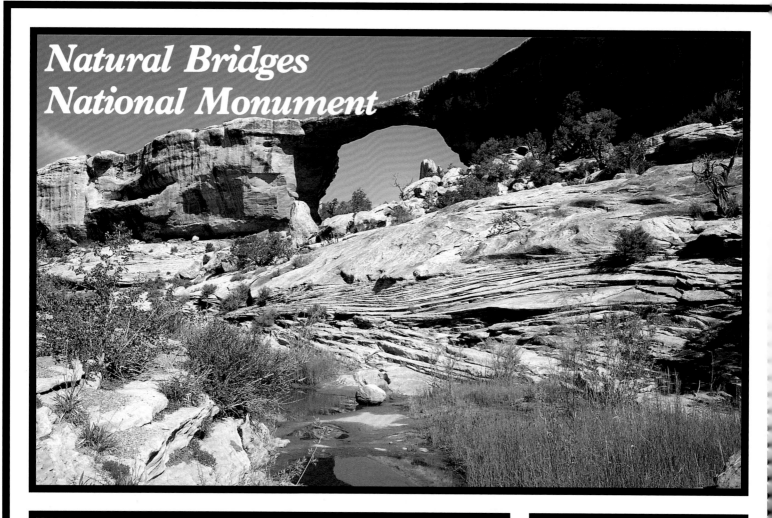

NATURAL BRIDGES NATIONAL MONUMENT is an area of Utah where the plateau has eroded into fantastic formations. Large bridges of rock are characteristic of this area.

Owachomo Bridge *(top left)* is about 10 million years old and is the oldest natural bridge in the area. Its salmon pink, 10-foot-thick span is 200 feet long and crosses over Armstrong Canyon at a height of 108 feet.

Kachina Bridge *(lower left)* is larger and darker than the other bridges in the Monument. It is over 107 feet thick and with a 186-foot-span, towers 205 feet above the canyon below.

CAPITOL REEF NATIONAL PARK is a sort of centerpiece to the Waterpocket Fold, a flexure or upthrust of the earth's crust, about 100 miles long. Capitol Reef itself is essentially a ridge or cliff face about 20 miles long. Its spectacle combines the monumental granduer of Zion with the bizarre fantasies of Bryce.

Chimney Rock *(top right)* is located 3 miles west of Fruita, between Richfield and Green River.

Hickman Bridge *(bottom right)* was formed by stream erosion in creamy colored Navajo Sandstone. It is 117 feet high and has a span of 137 feet.

The Egyptian Temple location *(top middle)* is another example of the spectacular results of wind, rain, and stream erosion in the Park.

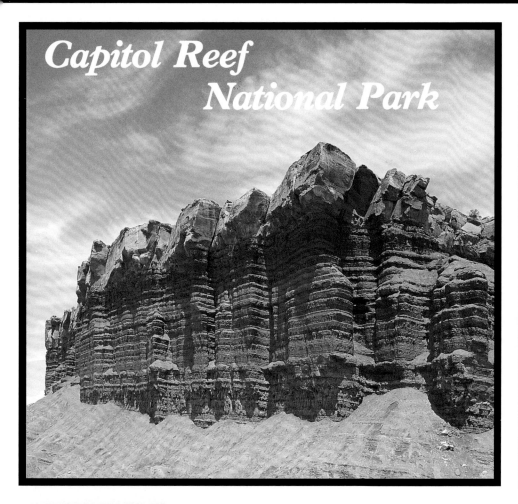

Capitol Reef
National Park

Red Canyon

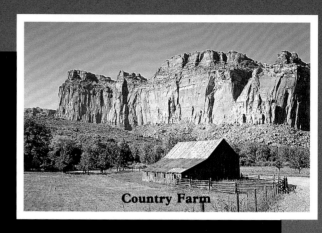

Country Farm

Autumn Splendor

Goblin Valley

Cedar Breaks National Monument

46

COLOR COUNTRY, Wind water and millions of years have eroded Southern Utah's redrock into massive Gothic walls and columns, Sphinx-sized statuary and lacy gingerbread trimming.

COLOR COUNTRY has provided the backdrop for numerous Hollywood classics, including "Drums Along the Mohawk" and "The Electric Horseman".

Bryce Canyon National Park

Left:
It's only Limestone, carved by rain, frost and running water, but the forms strike the imagination and produce such wonders as the vivid Canyon Walls pictured here.

Top: Queen's Castle
One of the countless castles, spires, temples and towers in this water-eroded limestone landscape, the Queen's Castle is located on the ¾ mile self-guided Queen's Garden Trail, descending 320 vertical feet below Sunrise Point to the reigning Victoria.

Bottom: Winter at Bryce Canyon
Snow cover contrast with the vivid colors. Winter is a beautiful time to see the main canyon.

Ages of erosion have carved the limestone plateau at Bryce into colorful steeples and amazing designs. This artist's paradise has often been called "The Ancient Sculptor's Workshop". From 1830 to 1850 the area was visited by adventurous trappers and prospectors. The canyon was later named for Ebenezer Bryce who settled near its mouth in 1875.

Top: Boat Mesa and the Queen's Garden
This view from Sunset Point presents a small part of the Bryce formations. Paiute Indians called it "Red-rocks-standing-like-men-in-a-bowl-shaped-canyon".

Bottom: The Silent City from Inspiration Point
The softer portions of stone have eroded leaving an array of endless towers, spires, minarets and sheer walled fortresses in strange and weird formations.

Top:
Within the 56-square mile area of Bryce Canyon National Park stands the jagged edge of Paunsaugunt Plateau. Here are exposed the famous Pink Cliffs of Bryce Canyon, carved in Wasatch limestone. These rock sculptures challenge the imagination not only with their fantastic forms, but with their color, a riot of pink and red and orange blended with white, gray, and cream. Here and there strips of lavender, pale yellow, and brown appear — threads of color gone astray from the master design.

Bottom: Thor's Hammer
Thor's Hammer and many other brilliantly colored pinnacles are viewed with awe by those who visit Bryce Canyon National Park, one of the world's most colorful Canyons.

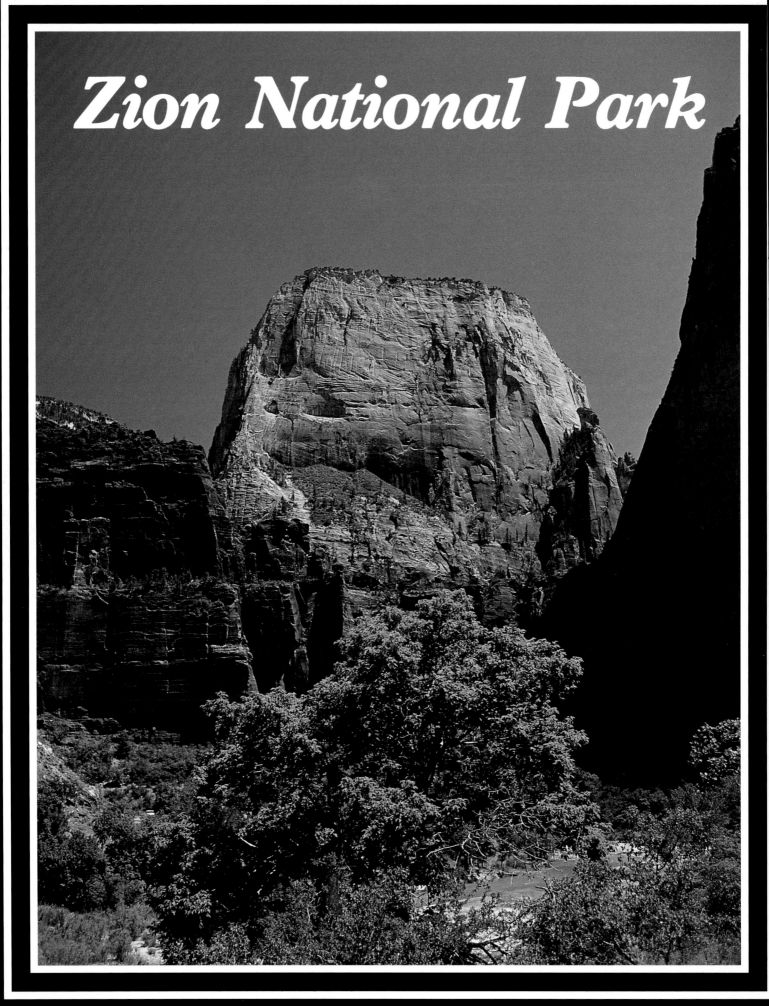

Zion National Park

Left:
The Great White Throne is the most famous point in Zion. The sheer stone walls, of this spectacular mountain rise 2,447 feet above the floor of the canyon.

Top:
The 'Sentinel' can be seen from the west portal of the Zion Tunnel. The tunnel was completed in 1930. Its total length is 5,607 feet. The Mount Carmel Highway that connects Int. 15 (Hiwy 91) and U.S. 89 is truly a remarkable scenic road. This highway also runs through the Park and the famous Zion Tunnel.

Bottom: Checkerboard Mesa, Mt. Carmel Highway — The Mt. Carmel Highway is 11.5 miles in length. It extends east from the Virgin River Bridge in Zion Canyon, up a series of switchbacks, and thru the famous tunnel with windows, where the galleries afford colorful panoramas of the canyon. At the eastern end, is the Checkerboard Mesa — giant cones of unusual and fantastically colored formations.

An area of great natural temples and cathedrals, Zion's inspiration is reflected in the names given its peaks. Here mountains are called temples, patriarchs, thrones and cathedrals.

Twenty miles of roads and a network of footpaths and horse trails lead to the attractions in Zion Park. Especially popular with the motorist is the drive up the floor of the main canyon.

Top: Switchbacks, Mt. Carmel Highway — Running east and west forming a link between highways 89 and 91, this road is considered a remarkable engineering feat. Winding through canyons of spectacular formation, the road descends to the canyon floor through a tunnel 5,607 feet long. Picture windows carved at intervals overlook sheer canyon walls and a series of six major switchbacks.

Bottom: The Great Arch from the Switchback Road. — This beautiful arch was developed by seepage of ground water along planes of crossbedding in the Navajo sandstone. Water dissolves the cementing material from the sandstone and causes masses of rock to fall away.

Top: Kolob Canyons Area
A highway makes accessible to the motorist the spectacular Kolob Fingers Canyons of the Zion National Park, located adjacent to Interstate 15 between Cedar City and St. George, Utah. This scenic wilderness area is ideal for photographers, picnickers, hikers and horseback parties.

Bottom: West Temple and Altar of Sacrifice
This view from near the Visitor Center is one of Zion's best. The West Temple towers nearly 4,000 feet above the valley floor. The Altar of Sacrifice has been colored by iron oxide stains dripping down its white face from the Temple Cap member.

UTAH — FALL COLORS
Scenic fall colors in the canyons of Utah are not easily forgotten.